FEARLESS FLOWER

SABREENA YASEEN

ISBN 979-888546969-2

Contents

Contents

Foreword

The book is about the journey of a girl, who has faced certain incidents in her childhood and suffered the consequences. She recalls her different stages of adolescence and have narrated the same by applying the technique "Stream of consciousness". The book contains certain elements of prose and poetry as well. The author has written about the difficult phases of teenage, and how important it is to tackle with them in a right manner. She has thoroughly mentioned how necessary it is, to be under the supervision and guidance of our parents and elders. She requests to the parents, guardians, elders and siblings out there, to understand their children and youngsters. She focusses to maintain a cordial relationship with each other in order to bridge the gaps and barriers. She points out how an adolescent becomes a victim, slips from the right track, clings to nasty habits and wears a rude attitude. She once and again, warns and advices the youngsters to save themselves from these activities. She elaborates how the physical and psychic changes affect the all around development of a teenager. Hence, she points out, how necessary it is for an individual to stay careful during this phase and how important it is for their elders to co-operate with them. She discerns how people around are evil doers and cannot be your well wishers always. She talks about her emotional breakdown and how she conquers it back with the help of her family and k2 academy. This book has certain poems under the title of Challenge, Deceive, Love, Dark-nights, Rejection, Academy, Parents, Classroom etc. In these poems, she have used free verses reflecting the free flow of emotions in her. She has written about the people, who had impacted her negatively and positively as well. The poem 'Gang' mentions how beautifully she had enjoyed her time with friends. She reminisces the fun games they used to play together and how skillfully they have managed the ups and downs in their friendship. This poem stays in contrast with the poem 'Friends', where in the last stanza, she writes how at the certain point of time, her friends became rivals and a threat to her success. She uses the regular refrain in this particular poem 'I hark back those days', discerning how the days have changed something out of her. The two more poems, that stay in contrast are 'Love' and 'Deceiveness'. In the poem Love, the poet talks about the single sided love. She talks, about the connection that she felt in teenage, is still clutched to her somewhere. She couldn't forget that special feeling, which the opposite person murdered. She remembers how still in her youth, that intensity didn't die. Despite all this, she couldn't forget the lessons that she learnt out of it. In the poem 'Deceiveness', she directly asks to the person, how his deceiveness had brought pain, tears and sadness in her life. She points out that she couldn't either forget or forgive him as he had teared her apart. The poem has certain examples of oxymoron like ' you put these crucial times in my hands as a gift' or 'you make me incomplete'. Other poems that stay in contradiction are 'Rejection' and 'Hope'. The poem 'Rejection' summarizes how the poet broke down due to certain rejections. These rejections had impacted her badly like her dreams ended, her hopes ruined, her passion got wrecked and how her goals reached to an end. The refrain 'i hate you alot' clues to what extent the poet had been disturbed by certain rejections. She makes use of Simile by directly comparing certain rejections to ruiner and destructor. In the poem 'Hope', she thoroughly refers it as a Saviour. The author mentions how hope in the later phase of adolescence, has been a map, which has directed her to the right path. She mentions it as her partner that has helped her to tackle the hard times. She makes use of Simile again and directly mentions hope as a protector, shield and sword. It has assisted her to assimilate the wreckage caused by rejections.

Her poems are usually without any rhyme scheme and runs from four stanzas to five stanzas. The diction is simple and beautiful. This book is suitable to any age group as it thoroughly collects the phases of childhood, encountered by everyone of us.

Foreword By:

Saraf Ali Bhat

Preface

The book is about the experiences of a teenaged girl who faces different stages of life. The book has been written to convey a message to all the parents to understand their children and guide them so that they would not astray. The children should be kept under the shadow of the elder ones and they need to spent their time with their family and understand the societal skills of the world.

Sabreena yaseen

Acknowledgements

Let me thank you all for spending your precious time in reading my book. It was a dream for me to publish a book and which came true due to the benevolence of Almighty and keen support of my nears and dears.

Digital Distribution.

Publishing-in-support-of,

sarafali.in
The voice of unpublished writings.

Mohalla Sultanpura, opp partap exclusive hostel Wali Gali, main stop Janipur, Jammu - 180007
Facebook: Saraf Ali Bhat | sarafali101@gmail.com

Book published and managed on digital stores by ***sarafali.in***

I get stimulated with an anecdote of a sixteen year old girl, who tries to forward a message to every individual "Be the Revolution" and is the slogan of her life. Her message to each teenager is that realize your self, stop avenue on individuals. If you want to be the buttress of your family begin from now. If you can control your teenage reactions, you will be the revolution. Its time to change the mindset of people because everything occurs in mind. If you learn to take everything positive from childhood, you will be a positive thinker in future. Life teaches us a lot and if we memorize the lessons , we will never get down or let any one down. Each step of existence is not hard but there is something in each step which says to us that "You have still to do more". The girl usually says that I am grateful to world that they realize me as I am! She requests to every teenager that if your parents set you free, give you liberty, don't do that things which make them feel excrucisted and scorn. She silicate to each children , who are in teenage or who have to enter in teenage that kindly stop misdemeanor. She openly dissipates her message that If today you want to change the society, change the mindset of individuals. By doing so, there will be an ease for new generation to tackle the tough time of teenage. If today you assist a girl in her mission to change the world, I believe there will be a revolution soon because your one right step can brought a great change in mankind.

Teenage : A stage where everything change whether our emotions, proclivity, assimilation, or duty. Only the thing is that we have to assimilate this age. We have to face new things like mood swings and is the most difficult part of this stage. During this stage there are some changes due to hormones in our body both internal and external, as well. Mostly things change, like our view of thinking, change in our personality, change in our way of speaking etc. The most salient thing is that this is the phase, where we choose our destiny because here, we get a chance to know about ourselves, to know about the capacities, capabilities, strengths, weaknesses and much more. The habits that we adopt here stay whole life with us. So try to take this stage seriously because this is where our personality begins to develop.

The girl is so disrupt and melancholic because the deadly nightmare has ruined her peace. The only question of her mind is, why my hallucination betrayed me? No one has a befitting reply to this question because it was not only that nightmare which betrayed her but every single person whom she trust, left her betrayed. During this crucial time, she got aware about her querido who are like cat and dog with her. Every one is against her. Today even her stickability is not with her. She can't manifest her fondness because she is in bad condition. People hate her because of her haughtiness. Her stickability is against her because of her self-conceit.

She is a dagio losing everything by her haughty, cynicism and self-conceit. At times, she say to people that you are grasping, and stay that time only when your behoof is, you are all iffy. She even lose her gaiety. A time came, when a boy (best friend) appeared in her life. He assimilated her fondness, anger, mind and everything. The girl became addicted to him, and people believe that he will became the reason of her swap. A time came when the best friend left her by saying "you are not erroneous and bad only and the thing which is iffy is your ego, dim view. I tried to replace that but you don't want to change. If you are happy with it, live with it, but I can't stay with you now. He added "change yourself before you lose yourself". This all had no effect on her but she missed him everyday even every second but never confessed. Time passed, she is still walking in the circle of self-conceit and cynicism but she never felt it. She was losing herself because she never used to feel herself, understand herself. The evocation in her mind is fade now as she never live that evocation after stepping in circle of ego and attitude. Now its tough to take her reward from that level but miracles happen everyday. A marvel betide on her birthday as she became successfully in taking her stickability back. Almost after one year, she stepped out from the world of inventiveness to the reality. During this year, lot of things changed but she was unaware like the way people now used to think about her. Now she has to face a lot of things and was not in that condition. She has to fight firstly with herself so that she can achieve herself and then with people to change their mind set. She has to face all that things which she used to do with people. She now hark back the last words of her best friend who was in her life. Before one year she realized that the boy said right but couldn't employ it in her life. She regrets that if she has acted the way, he said, things had been better now.

She is now totally faded about her past. She miss her childhood, where she used to be favourite of everyone. She assisted, esteemed all and sundry. she miss that time when she used to sleep peacefully, go to school calmly, meet her friends desperately, study solemnly, play happily and remembers how she used to come with soiled uniform, gruppy shoes and with mucky hands. She missed those days when she used to be the leader of her gang, captain of school team, C.R of class, best articulator of class, best player of school and a student who always used to irritate her younger ones. But she only hark back the habits but not the moments which she used to live. Also she has to cross her teenage because she was in the mid of the teenage. She has to face all that mood swings, change in body, change in weening, change in way of enunciating, change in disposition, change in all over life. She feel like she was nab in dark room where there is no ray of light but she has to find that ray of light because she has to overcome from that darkness, so that she can find herself. She used to spent her dark nights in thinking who changed me? Who borrowed me here? Who make my past faded for me? Who gave me strength to change? Who captured me in this darkness? Who ruined my dreams? Who took my passion? Who broke my trust? What made me wrost in front of Individuals? Who made me cheater? Who made me a liar? Who took my life away from me? Who captured my happiness? Who made me reckess? Who ruined my life? What is the reason behind this all? And Who will enlighten my life now??

With these questions she spent three years of her teenage . In these three years, she always ask a question to herself that who was the reason behind that all? And who will make her life enlighten now? After three years, she got an answer that the reason behind that all was just herself and only she can enlighten herself again. After getting an answer, she become silent for a long time and spent life with one more question that how can i find myself again? Her birthday came and that day one more miracle happened, she got an answer of one more question. She comprehended that yes.. You will find yourself but you have to change yourself first, that time she was about fourteen years means a student of 8th standard. A crucial time came means now she realize there are changes in her body, in way of thinking, in way of talking, and in everything. She was facing mood swings, by then she put herself separate and she feel alone among thousands of people.. She felt separated because her thinking change, and understood that these all these things which she felt or which are going on, are effects of teenage over her. She took the biggest step of her life and went to search herself!

And she goes like she was never here!!!!!!

1

Gang.

That silence when I used to come,

That noise when i used to stay, That gathering when I used to leave,

All is done with you!

That decision by which you all agree,

That rules which you all follow

That talks which you all used to do,

All is done with you!

There might be difference, There might be an argue, There might be up down in our relations,

All is done with you!

I hark back that days,

When we used to do water fighting,

When we used to do ink fighting, When we used to do painting on uniforms,

All is done with you!!!

I hark back that moments,

When we used to play red hand in class,

When we used to play kho -kho in class,

When we used to play ice–water in

class,

All is done with you!

Our gang was best and most powerful gang in the school, but time parted us from each other!!!!

I really miss you all !

2

Dark Nights.

The most worst nights,
The most crucial nights,
The most restless nights,
The most overthinked nights,
Its you dark nights!
The most memorable nights
The most learned nights
The most hurted nights The most failure nights,
Its you dark nights!
You are most important part of my
life
You are most favorite part of my
life
You are most wounded part of my life
Because you make me that which no one expect.
Its you dark nights!
You mean all to that's why you are most favourite and least hated part.
Only you dark nights....

Her first day was not good on that route because she was unaware about the rules and regulations of that route. she used to spend her most time in loneliness, where she only thought, how she can change herself or what she has to change? The second day was a little better because she was now understanding the rules and regulations. Day by day she became aware about all rules and regulations ..she was too near to herself but like miracles betide everyday, an incident also happen everyday. One more incident takes place in her life, which pulls him so far from her. This time she was not wrong but people were. She never used to break trust of people but this time people broke her trust. Actually the incident was, the image she create before four years in individuals mind was still like that. People didnt understand the changes which she has undergone now but they only remember the weird behaviour in her which betides before four years. A group of people start taking revenge and their was no limit in their revenge. The Shocking news for the girl was that the leader of that group was her best friend ... That day, she snivel a lot because a biggest flood has occurred in her life, her childhood best friend was against her. Dear reader, have you faced the same situation somewhere in your life?

She wanted to give up but this time, its about not about winning or losing. If she gives up this time, she would entirely separate from her spirit. That day she learn, people were never loyal including her chums. She stood against her best friend in a hope that her best friend will change and support her. A time came, when her friends and the people known to her were against knowing the fact that she has changed and this all happened because of her best friend only. By this incident her hope get diminished. She was going slowly too far from herself. Her support, strength everything seemed declining. The true faces of the people and their reality unveiled before her. She wanted to know everything truth and reality at this time as she knew if once she get wrecked, it would take time to get the broken self repaired.

3

Best Friend

Abandon world believe!
Sometime you are a sister,
Sometime you are a secretbox
Sometimes you are a sibling,
Its time to say, What you were,
What you are, what you will!
Because you have still lot of phases!
A phase, where you are only my friend
A phase, where you are only my best friend
A phase, where you are only my sibling
I'm still unaware about you!
A time, when you support me a
lot,
A time, when you love me a lot
A time, when you care for me a lot
I'm still unaware about you!
One thing i want to say about you
One phase I want discuss about you
One time i want to elaborate about you,
I'm still unaware about you!
Sometime you are my biggest enemy,

Sometime you are my biggest competitor,
Some time you are my biggest hater.
Here I completely know You!

4

Friends.

I hark back those days! When we used to play together, hen we used to eat together, hen we used to walk together,

When we used to stand together

But people make us apart!!

I hark backthosedays!

When we used to be in one team

When we used to be one in front of individuals,

When we used to be one in front of rivals,

When we used to be one in font of teachers, But people broke our unity!!

I hark back those moments!

When we used to play as one against boys,

When we used to play as one against seniors,

When we used to play as one against rivals,

When we used to play as one against classmates,

But people snatch our strength!

I hark back those days too!

When you all was against me,

When you all became my biggest rival

When you all became my biggest threattomy goal When you all became my biggest speedbreakertomy goal

Because people make you so!

It's a great chance for the haters to have an attack on her, to make her loser, to make her failure, to make her weaker, to demolish her and all goes the same. Their initial attack was to make her weak, then failure, loser and then try to demolish her, but their last throw missed the target and they remain Unsuccessful in their mission. The thing was that they demolish her more than half and that was the

Knotty. There is a solution, but that's tough, full of obstacles, hurdles which was impossible to cross. She tried her best to bring him back but her inner will was killed somewhere. After six months ,her inner will became successful to bring him back from the level of demolishing. Now, she was slowly coming back to her form. This time there is a great revolution. This time she know that there will be haters, rivals, liars but she has to face all of them. This Chance was the last chance to achieve herself, to fulfil her wishes and to complete her dreams and to achieve her goal. She has to take risk, to be proud on herself. She has to face hurdles, to be unfearable because she was the backbone, supporter and a protector of her family. She was prepared now for all challenge's, exams, hurdles, obstacles and pain. She was only thinking that she has to achieve herself, to Change herself, to change the thinking of people and all that. She take a step to her goal with full enthusiasm. She leave her wishes, habits, dream, aim everything only for herself.

In teenage, facing this all is to much difficult for a teenager. It takes time to understand anything because during teenage lot of things underwent change. Losing friend, best friend or supporters in teenage means a lot. Taking decision, living alone, fighting alone is very tough for teenager. If anyone deceives a teenager, that thing pushes him/ her hard and backward and becomes difficult to comeback on a right track. So yes, this is a fragile stage, where things needed to be handled carefully.

Dear reader, could you reminisce your mistakes as a teenager? The only thing, this girl has to do is that she has to fight now and she give up, then her whole life she will be incomplete. She begins to fight for herself. Her best friend and now a rival don't leave any moment to irritate her. She was distracting him for her goal. The girl became a bit weak everyday because everyday she has to fight with her best Friend. This is cumbersome for her, as this relation meant a lot to her and all that moments and memories she experienced with him were rewinding in her mind. A biggest shock came to her. She lose her every single supporter, and saw herself faded. The last ray she had was just the hope and she hope for the best. She hold the hand of the hope and walk with it. She has to become complete because her responsibilities are waiting.

Hey teenager, realize a thing, hope is the only thing, which make impossible things possible any moment. Don't leave the hand of hope, because its not only hope, it's a way to your goal, which can make you successful, so never lose it!!

Holding your hand,
Walking your way,
Seeing your miracle,
Following your rules,
I get faded!
Cant handle myself,
Can't lose myself
You are the road, so to take me up, I get faded! In the road of cumbersome, Thanks for been my partner.
hanks for been my second half.
Thanks for been my smile.
I get faded!
In the way of war,
Thanks for been my shield,
Thanks for been my protector,
Thanks for been my sword, I get faded!
Thanks for being always there, dear hope!

A day came, when her struggle change into an achievement. She finds herself in a lot of cumbersome. Today her ego, attitude every thing gets demolish because she now wanted to be happy and kind.

Dear teenager, f you want to be unique, so come out of your comfort zone. You have an ideal but did you ever think that how that person became ideal of people? Let me tell you, he/she became ideal due to his/ her achievement, struggle, and hard work. You chose your ideal, so that you can be like him/her, follow his/her everything, every habit, every action but you never want to struggle like him, you never do hard work like him as you only want to be like your ideal but never the ideal. Here you do a mistake, you start your journey to be unique but While walking in the journey, you become a follower. You became follower because you sometime lose the trust on yourself, you sometime forget why did you come out from the bed of roses. To be ideal, leader, or boss is not a cake walk. Some time you have to leave your own will to achieve something, sometime you have to leave your comfort zone to be something, sometime you have to adjust to learn something. Your ideal have done this all that's why he/she is today a role model. Hey teenager stop being copy cat, be something different. Create your own rules, make your own way, achieve your own goal, stop walking like role model or ideal.

Be unique, be different!

"In the desire to touch sky, don't be the bird Be the one, so that sky have a desire to touch you"

The girl do the same mistake as every teenager do. She decided to be different and unique from the world but when she walk on the road, instead to be a leader, she became a follower. When she took first step towards the road she doesn't know this way will not be a cake walk. She wants to be different and unique but in her comfort zone. As I have already discussed that to be unique we have to come out from the comfort zone, we have to the leave the luxurious life. We have to do struggle, hard work to be unique. A thing happen, she got an opportunity to play Martial Arts. She went for the national and it was her first national level who she was going to play. In this tour, she learned alot. She learned the importance of hard work and leaving the comfort zone. She get to know about people's nature, experienced new things, new people and new places. She learn how to adjust, how to forgive, how to apologize and why these things are important. She won the gold medal there She don't only come with a gold medal but with a lot of experience, and exposure. That time with her were two things, first her teenage and second her desire. We know teenage effects are worst one but If we can't handle it carefully, we will leap high.

6

Desire.

You borrow me from the sky,
You put me on the ground,
You took me from the dust,
You hold me on the peak,
Because I believe and you do! You hold me in the dark nights,
You hold me in the crucial days,
You hold me in the restless months,
You hold me in the overthinked year
Because i believe and you do!
You took me from that depth where no one reach
You took me from that incident which i never forget
You took me from that flood which snatch my everything
You took me from that level which only gives wound
Because I believe and you do!
You put me away from the individuals,
You put me together with my heart,
You put me away from those faded memories,
You put me together with my own self Because I believe and you do!

You borrow me from that level where i give up
You took me from that level where I deceive myself
You hold me at that level where a person wants to suicide
You put me at that level where only people' s hope reach but can't people
Because you believe and I do!

She prepares herself only to achieve that goal, only to fulfil her desire, only to change her dream into reality. She is literally unknown from the upcoming hurdles, obstacles and many other things. The first step of her towards her goal and first hurdle and speed breaker in that road demotivate her, breaks her confidence because it was first rejection of her life. She was rejected just in first step and in her first try. Everything look impossible to her. . She kept quiet for a long time thinking why her every trial faces failure, why she get rejected in every step, what is the reason? Without losing her hope she continued to fight for herself, continuously putting her steps forward, challenged every rejection. She lost her every challenge but every morning she was ready to face something new. She usually said "I'm fed up of losing, giving challenges, I want now something new which will be different, competitive, strong and of same standard" I want something which will enforce me to change myself and to achieve my goal. She is unaware that there are many things, lot of people who will be her biggest competition. There are different type of people, different type of obstacles, hurdles and speed breakers. She think this is ending without knowing that this was not film, this is just a trailer. She cross the trailer and puts step in this on going film, where she saw different things, unique people and much more. She was continuously walking on that road facing everything, her life was in cumbersome but she smile because she don't know at last she has to face a biggest shock and a biggest defeat. At the end of that road, she face a different toughest, hardest speed breaker and that speed breaker was her friends. They are trying to take her at the bottom , her friends are playing role of snake. Everything end there, not any success, any goal nothing matter to her that time. She was confused why they both are doing this to her and if friends can't see her at top, she can understand their insecurities but what those who support them ?? Why they were trying to mix my hard work with dust? She give her every happiness, every thing to the martial arts.

She sacrificed her studies for that game. She has make that game first priority of her life . Her game is every thing to her and her coach knew this all. She was now disturbed by the question, why now this attack at all? But she couldn't find the answers and left playing the game. She can't be happy without the game, still left everything related to the game. After five months, she re-joined the game but under different Coach. Those five months, she only think why that happen? But never get any answer. But the memories, attachment, bonding with the game and with the people who are in game brought her back. Yes! She joined the game but now she has only fear that if this coach do the same, then what will happen because she was only under different coach but in same academy. Almost after one year she leave that Coach and that academy. She hold the hand of a great person, whom she call" farzan sir". He was the person who love her like his daughter, teach her like his sister and the girl always say that under his shadow, she was comfortable and safe. She was in a team whom she cal l"k2 academy", where she got her brother and friends. She was thankful to

God that she got an academy which is the best and the coach, great. Her team was always with her, they never leave her alone, support her in every path of her life and love her the most. After going in the k2 academy, she never fight alone but always fight with her team against every cumbersome. She completed her first goal which was to get under the coach who have a great heart and to play within a team where players have a bond more stronger than blood relations.

Hey teenager! Did you face anything like this, where you get pushed down by your loved ones.

If yes, so you are the one among brilliant minds because people always pushed those who are at the top. Let this situation be handled with calmness, leave not your goal, but make it your target.. Hey teenager, you have the power that if you want, you can be at the top in teenage.

The girl has crossed first phase of teenage. A phase where a person only gets an introduction of anything. She has now a team which will support her but the team can only support her but can't fight at her place. She has to fight alone in her next phase. The second phase of teenage is full of Cumbersome, it is a phase where a person get tempted easily, where a person get an attachment with wrong things easily, where teenager mostly fall in love, where a teenager mostly choose wrong way, Where a teenage mostly deceive herself. It's a stage where mood swings have the most important role. A teenager can't understand her mood swings, can't handle the fury, hateness, wound given by the mood swings. In this stage, boys get an attachment with wrong things, sometime with wrong people. They used to take drugs, smoking and other wrong activities. Some boys get attached with the fashion trends. They used to spend money of their parents in buying clothes, other accessories. They used to follow fashion and other things to that level that they ignore their studies. This stage effect a lot in boys life. In this stage, girls has to face lot of cumbersome, new things and new changes. They get new things to know, to experience, to realize, new changes to accept. In this stage, teenage girls have to face a lot because they cant easily adjust their self in this. They get afraid when there is change in their body, they afraid to told it to their parents. The pain, the changes, the mood swings and other things confused them. In the initial, they can't bear the pain of periods, can't bear the irritation of it, cant bear the mood swings that come in period. The changes which occur in their body are new by which they get afraid, start feeling uncomfortable, can adjust themselves in new place. They start feeling shy as same as boys, they also get diverged to wrong things, wrong activities and wrong people. Hey teenager! Everyone who is in this stage get diverged, but after diversion you have to make that diversion a right path for yourself. You can't deceive yourself, your dreams, your parents, you have to be loyal, so to be loyal you have to start understanding this age. Yaah! Its difficult to control yourself, your mood swings and other activities but you have at least try to make the diversions a right path. It's tough sometime or impossible to make it right.

But hey teenager you have to face this all because if you lose from this so how can you win the challenges of rest of the life. "you are the warrior and warriors never lose" Remember this dear always.

Where the worlds nightmare end, Your life starts from there!!!

The girls has to face second phase of life which is too tough. She understands that this phase is going too hard than any other. When she see the days of periods, she get afraid, hesitates to tell these things to her mother or sister. She feel shy, ashamed because she thinks it's wrong. She can't bear the pain, she used to cry whole day and used to awake whole night. She feels insecure and get shocked when these things in reality happen with her. She want to cry loudly so that her heart get a piece of relief. But after all, as every teenager do she do the same. She get diverged to a path. She falls in love, the feeling she had that time is different. This time she was in love with a beautiful soul . Yaah! She has fallen in love before this but now she was in an imaginary live . She think that this is different from everything. She started making every right thing wrong, start ignoring her studies and she used to spend time with her love. By this she forgot that she had walked a long distance and has still to cover a lot. She involved deeply with her love, forgetting her goal, aim, wishes everything. Now nothing mean for her except her love. Everyday she slips deep and agrees love change her life. In another way she deceives herself, she deceives her dream, her goal especially herself. She break limit in love without any hesitation but soon she realize she was doing wrong and this happens because of her growing mentality . which indirectly teach her that involving in love relationship is nothing but goal, dream, wishes, studies to a student, everything. She left the love relationship not because that the beautiful soul deceive her because she feel she is deceiving herself. Breaking relation of two years is not tough but breaking a relation which is different, whose feelings are different, whose meaning is different, whose memories are different, whose destination is different, a bond in which a person makes thousand of memories, hundred of moments which a person never forget is hard. She has a different attachment with that relation which she can't left. This time she not only deceive herself but also a soul who love her a lot. She wanted to be Loyal in this bond. She as always believe in fortune or destiny and that day her fortune show a miracle. The boy deceived her because she doesn't want a partner who has to do struggle for every moment, who is boring, who don't know how to stay in bond. The things which boy say that day hurts the girl most, the boy crosses every limit but the girl only said "I believe in fortune. If you would be in my destiny, you would come back" I gave you my time, my life and my everything. It didn't mean what I get back but what I learn. You want to leave so here is full freedom to you because I'm enough strong to handle myself. You are saying that I was boring, let me tell you I was not boring, just your thinking is old. You complained to me that I don't know about bonds, so listen i have the bonds which are more special than you and the moments, memories we have lived I'm freeing you from that all. Live your Life if you can and hark, a day come when you will be one of them who are my follower and a biggest fan, just remember.

“Waqt tou apna khel dikha chuka hai,

Sabr, ab bari terii khel ki hai".

She has to start everything from beginning because team is busy in now making an academy. Family is busy In making relations. Siblings are busy in making future and girl is confused in her future. She went back to her team leaving all confusion out of the door and start living in present.

She started focusing on her future. she started doing hard work for her future, to make her name.

She don’t need fame only but name, respect and proud.

She believe hard work has no end and destiny will never end!

Holding two rays of hope and walking in the road. She cry sometime a lot when she get rejected. she torcher herself a lot when she get rejected. Facing rejection, misbehaviour and all but she still walk. The destiny always play a game and this time destiny do the same, somebody hold her and promise her that never leave her. He supported her a lot, always encourage her, motivate her and most important love her. As she hold two rays, same two person’s hold her hand and make her comfortable at every level. One she call “bhai” another she call “coach”. Family was always with her in every little step, even that single thing of which she is afraid. But cumbersome don’t end there, they follow the way where the girl go like alittle baby, the cumbersome hold her finger and don’t want to leave. But the girl has to come out of these cumbersome and make herself. Love ,affection, bond, care anything doesn’t matter to her. Now taking an aim that she want now to be inspiration for other peoples especially teenagers, she want to share her experience with them. She want to share the situations she faced in life not any other teenager should face. It’s a stage where the incidents happen, and stories and miracles takes place.

She focus on her study and start entitling her name in toppers of the class .In her school life, she is also know n by one more name that’s most rude behavior girl. She also secure name in the field of Martial arts, As there was also a tag of rude behavior. The word rude kills her, hurt her every second but she get used to stay with it, to be happy with it. She saw a lot in the second phase of life like affection, Love, care, Deceiveness, diversions and much more. Also in second phase of her life, she also get addicted of wrong things and wrong bonds but with plenty of time she also get out of that bonds and things. She only want to forward a simple message to the teenager that its you who can make it a perfect and worst. All depend on you, I only recommend you that work on your future because when you will be something then you don’t follow world’s trend but you will became an ideal. Stop theseTyhings like following trends of world, following fashion, following an Ideal, to become addicted of wrong things. These all things give you nothing except waste your time, money ,knowledge, smile, moments and life. Enjoy your teenage, because it will never comeback, enjoy that masti which you do with your best friend, enjoy that fights which you do with your classmates, enjoy that matches which you play with your classmates, enjoy that moments when you taunt or irritate your school teacher with your friends. ,Enjoy that punishment which you get not on borrowing copy, enjoy that punishment which you get on making noise in class, disobeying the rules , not obeying the C.R of class , enjoy that moment when you do outdoor competition with your classmate , enjoy that moments which you spend with your teacher , seniors, juniors, enjoy your life ,enjoy your moment when you are called adolescent . Change now, the meaning of adolescent, be the change now . Borrow a trend of changing meaning of adolescent because then you will be treated still as a mature guy. Falling in love is a unpredictable thing but staying in love is something great because a person can fall in love with his/her game, aim, family, parents,books, goals and with much more. Put the negative thinking aside because this new generation want everything sorted, want everything tied together, happy and enjoyable. This generation want all relation happy and want everybody together. Hey teenager, you are the future of the nation if you become the revolution then the upcoming generation will be different.

"Be the reason of someone 'smile, if you can't, then don't be the reason of their tears"

Its now the last or third phase, where a different feeling have to face, a different attitude, a different personality, a different biography, a different introduction and a different Way of lifestyle. A stage where a person explores its talent and make that talent a goal, an aim, or a source of happiness for them.

What a person choose here, will stay with him/her forever. Here mostly thinking of person, personality, attitude comes out and people start knowing what you are, who you are, what was the past, what is the present and what will be the future, how much you can do, how much anyone can do for you, how you end a bond, why you exist and all that things.

Here you teach alot and learn a lot. It's the age from fifteen to nigh teen where a person decides his/her future, Chose personality and start making it.

"Have the dream to touch

sky, But when the dream is sky,

Instead of parrot

Be the eagle "

The days of the third phase are going good.The girl is happy that the cruciality of life has ended but this time one last incident changed her life. The incident takes place in a worst time, some one deceive her. Deceive her in a way where only tears left. This turns her life in a way that nobody want to talk to her. Every single person stands against her, like they have a one slogan and one motive that is to ruin the life of the girl. Some real faces or great faces come forward in support of her. This Deceiveness change her Life totally. she used to stay now alone in the world of imagination. She don't want to talk to people now.

She want now something different and she do that. She give her love, care, time, hard work, struggle, Strength, affection all to her goal and finally achieve that. she has an art of writing and after working on that she pen down her all feelings and share it to world. she shares her all the good and bad moments in the form of poetry and forward it to the world. She believe writing have a power of changing world. It can heal that wound which antibiotics and doctors can't. It can motivate that person who hope has died. It can give us justice on every important topic. It's not only pen, it's a weapon which can change world in some days. It's weapon which have a power to jot down the inner feelings of the person. She used to take advices from her loved ones about her art and used to apply them. Currently she is the co-author of two books and the author of this book. The girl is still playing Martial arts under Farzan Hussain.

She get two great things, one is her school"Arun Public High School" and another is her academy "j&k k2 martial arts academy". These two things support her a lot. She continue her journey with the new name of writer. She is also member of event managing company "chinar Nst".

Now for always she hold the hand of every trouble, cumbersome and success. Getting the experience of both failure and Winner. She forward some message to the world. After facing the both phases of life i.e success and failure . she feel that there is change in her attitude, thinking, dreams, personality and in much more. She want to say to the teenager that this age teach a lot and this age is the turning point of everyone's Life. A message for parents of teenager is that please understand what they want to say, support them When they need you, stop making issue or discussing topic in front of them, just make them feel that their family is together always. It is a message for elder ones that whether you are an elder brother or sister please try to understand your younger ones because they are suffering from a crucial time, try to understand their words , their reasons, support them because if you understand them they will talk about their problems, you have the experience of this age so, say them clearly about this age, try to mix them with a friendly nature not with people because they will get ruined by individual's advices. Give them a Space where they can feel their self, motivate them in every step of life, be their courage, be their strength because this crucial time stays for sometime in their life.

Its message for younger ones or the teenager and to the one, who have to step in this age, don't follow the ways, rules, regulations which are decided by people because what you got or what you face in that way you have to face that alone, no one will be there. Hey teenager understand the difference between present, past and future.

Past was , your present is your future will be your

Decide at once, what you have to concentrate on? on what you have to work hard, who will be your priority and what will be your goal. I only can give you one advice that concentrate and work hard on future and focus on present. Make future your first priority and remember the mistakes and lessons of your Past and start discussing the issues and problems of your life with your parents and elder ones. Don't shy in front of your parents. Stop being nervous to say problems to your parents because just your parents are your well-wishers.

Try to make your bond good with your family, believe in their decisions, follow their rules, apply their advices as they want you to achieve high. Set your own goal and walk on it!

Stop thinking about the world, friends, relatives and start believing in your self. Remember a thing in your life that one who leave your hand in hard times, forgive them but never forget them because if you both forgive and forget them then how will you learn a lesson? Forgive everyone but never forget that person because if anyone can break trust at hard times then he/she can do anything , anytime. Remember your own struggle, your parents struggle because your struggle will decide your goal and your parents struggle will decide your thinking. Hey teenager, believe in the decision of your loved ones because their every word is about your goodness. If you want, so you can be the one who Will support the girl in the mission of the revolution.. If you want you can be the revolution.

To be a hand in bringing a revolution is not a cake walk. It is a cumbersome one, because Its not a simple revolution. I and you are opposing the thinking of thousands of people, rules and regulations of our ancestors and many other things. Only the thing I want is that, change that side of your thinking. Change your mindset that a boy who used to wear weird dressing, used to stand on roadside is not a wrong guy, see the positive side of every person. You have the capacity to took a person from a wrong path to the right one. Leaving, ignoring or tolerating is not an option, you have to face this all. As same as 'a book is not judged by its cover'. We have to be the revolutionaries by changing the thinking of individuals, motivating those who are disappointed from the world, bringing out the hidden talents of youngsters. Thinking matters the most in life on every stage. It shows the character and personality of a person because what a person think he/she will apply the same in their self and inturn it carves out our personality. I have learned from someone that ,"Be positive, positivity will come back to you".

This book isn't any motivational book but the advice for the teenagers. I don't want to show my struggle, hard work and other things to the world. I only want that what I face in teenage, the mistakes I did during my teenage, the hardships I faced, any other wouldn't face..

7

Challenges.

I hark back those days

When I used to wipe the tears lonely

When I used to hear the pain lonely

When i used to motivate the mind lonely

When I used to heal the wound lonely Because these all things are your gift!

I hark back those days

When eyes were full of water,

When heart were full of feelings,

When mind was full of

question,

When body were full of nervousness Because these all these are your gift!

I hark back those days

When eyes used to ask questions,

When heart used to find peace

When the mind used to find answer

When body used to be uncomfortable

Because these all were your gift!

I hark back those days

When I used to clean my eyes lonely so that anyone couldn't see me crying

When I used to bear the painlonelysoanyonecouldn't seemewrecked

When I used to motivate the mind lonely so that anyone couldn't know how weak I'm,

When I used to heal the wounds lonely so anyone couldn't get how deep my wounds are,

Because hey challenge, you introduce me to a new world!!

8

Rejections.

In the initial stage of teenage,
Without knowing your origin,
Without knowing your meaning,
Without knowing your effects,
Without knowing your results, So I hate you a lot!
In the beginning of my teenage,
You change my thinking,
You wrecked my hopes,
You ruined my way,
You destruct my goal, So I hate you a lot!
In the mid of my teenage,
You parted me from myself,
You make me far from dream,
You make me apart from passion,
You make me far from love, So I hate you a lot!
In the end of the teenage,
You taught me, life is full of cumbersome.
You taught me, loneliness is the best.
You taught me, believing is the first attack.
You taught me, bond is gift of God.
So I still hate you!

Because you forget to teach me that individuals always deceive.

9

Deceiving.

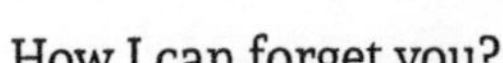

How I can forget you?
You are the most memorable,
You are the most special,
You are the most memorized,
Because you taught me the word that no one can't!
How I can forgive you?
You make me insecure,
You make me incomplete,
You make me imperfect,
Because you put me at that level where I cant find myself!
How you can be faded?
Did you hark back that wound?
Did you hark back that tears?
Did you hark back that pain?
What you borrow me as a gift!
How you can be favourite?
Didn't you remember, how loved ones apply you in my life?
Didn't you remember, how my dearest left me?
Didn't you remember, how I recognise the real faces?

You put these crucial times in my hands as a gift!
How I can forget you?
How I can forgive you?
How you can be faded ?
How you can be favourite ?

10

"Coach" (Dedicated to Mr Farzan Hussain)

Coach cum mentor,
Mentor cum head,
Head cum brother,
Brother cum life,
The one who plays thousand roles!
Sometime as the head of the family, Sometime as the coach of the team,
Sometime as the mentor of the student, Sometime as the shield of the army.
As a mentor,
Your words make us motivated.
Your actions make us ready.
Your tricks make us to win.
Your strategy make us players.
As a head,
Your points make us together.
Your smile make us happy.

Your presence make us stronger.
Your sacrifices make us champion.
As a brother and a life, Your advices become a ray of hope.
Your shadow become a refuge for me.
Your words become the way for me.
Your smile become the reason of my fight.
Because all the around, you are the best mentor!!

11

"Academy" (Dedicated to k2 Academy)

People call us academy, But we call ourselves family! People call us team-mates, But we call ourselves family members.

Here the world differs from k2!

We have the bond more stronger then best friends.

We have the bond more stronger then father and daughter.

We have the bond more amiable than mother and son.

We have the bond more sweeter then siblings.

Here the world differ from k2!

Talks here, are always different from the world.

Words shared, are different from world.

The protection here is different from the world.

The happiness spread here, is different from the world.

Here the world differ from k2!

Here i want to say to you all,

The most unique and special people of my life,

The most favourite people of my life,

The most strongest and motivated people of my life, The most important people of my life,

The people of k2,The people of k2!

12

LOVE

To this moment still,
I,
Can't forget that feeling
Cant describe that feeling
Can't destroy that feeling
Because it is related to someone different!
To this moment still,
You lived in the heart
You are missed in the breathes
You are loved in the prayers
Because you are now someone different!
To this moment still,
I can't forget those lessons,
I can't forget those morals,
I can't forget those mistakes,
Because you are now someone different!
To this moment still,
Never forgot you on my achievement,
Never forgot you on my victories, Never forgot you on my success, Because i am now someone different!

I did a mistake but never regret on that because the thing which taught me is a lesson to not mistake again!

13

Parents.

Parents are all about Mom and Dad,

Life is incomplete without both of them One is base, another is roof One is smile, another is happiness.

One is heartbeat, another is breath.

Both are important!

In the crucial days of my life,

I see my dad crying,

I see my mom suffering,

I see both of them in pain, I see both of them tense,

Because their child was in pain!

In the peaceful days of my life,

I see my dad happy,

I see my mom smiling,

I see both of them in peace, I see both of them worry free, Because their child is in peace !

You both are important.

Dad motivate me by his words,

Mom motivate me by her love,

Dad prepare me by his struggle,

Mom strengthens me by his patience, Because both are important!

Baat jab pyar ki hona, Ammi sai zada pyar Baat jab saath ki hona ,Baba sai zada saath ay mursheed ! Nai koye krta hai, na koye daitai hai!

14

Behna

A bond which tie me together to the love,

A bond of life, which tie me to myself, A bond of trust which tie me together to my heart,

A bond of faith, which tie me together to my soul

Here all bonds differ from you!!

The one who cry in my pain,

The one who smile in my peace,

The one who sneivel at my failure,

The one who laugh at my success, Here all bonds differ from you!

People say, three bodies and three souls, I say three bodies and one soul. People say, three goals and three warriors, I say three goals and one warrior. People say three daughter's and their mom, I say three son's and their queen. People say three loads and their dad, I say three supporters and their king.

Here the world differ from you

We were once in failure, We are one in success We were one in the dukedom we will be one until death make us separate.

Here the world differ from you!!

15

Bond.

I don't know where the bond start,

I don't remember when I and you convert into us. I don't remember when we start living in each other, I don't remember when we get to know each other.

It's a bond, where world became aside!

We are not friends

We are not siblings

We are not best friends

We are not cousins

It's a bond, where world became aside!

Just one phone call

Juts one minute talk Just one laughing word Pull the whole conversation so long.

It's a bond, where world became aside!

My angry face and your laughing face

My harsh mood and your chilly mood My tense looks and your worry free looks

Always collide together and make our day.

It's a bond, where world became aside!

My angry mood on your late entry

My happy mood, on picking call on the first ring My loved mood on your satisfication My harsh mood on your ruining the fixed plan.

It's a bond, where world became aside!
Wo kehta hai aj kal badi muskuranai lagai ho
Mursheed ! MalOom nhi usa
Hamay hamaray jaisa koye mil gaya hai!!!(BattErY)

16

Relation.

From childhood to this moment

We have the bond same

We have the trust same We have the love same We have the affection same,

Because the two sided remain same!!

We start from strangers,

Then became friends,

We continue as bestfriends At

this moment we are partners.

Because the two sided remain same!

Time parted us but the trust level always remain same, Words make us different but our love level always remain same, Situation make us far but our affection level always remain same.

Because the two sided remain same!

We both follow our destiny but never became apart, We both follow our dreams but never became far, We both follow our passion but never became apart,

Because the two sides remain same!

You hold the guitar and found peace in the tune of strings.

The tune of strings always show your pain.

The tune of strings always show your struggle.

The tune of strings always show your passion. The tune of strings always show your

talent

Because the two sided remain same! I never mean what people talk about you, because I know you since the childhood!!

Bless up singer(furiii)

17

Classroom.

That torcher zone of four walls,

That masti zone of four walls,

That hesitation zone of four walls, That irritating zone of four walls, By the way, it's my classroom!

Before the first bell, It is a play ground It is a hang out zone.

It is a discussion place,

By the way, it's my classroom!

After the first bell,

It automatically became a law room.

It automatically became a silent place. It automatically became a fighting ground.

By the way, it's my classroom!

In the mid of the day,

It became a lawless room where everyone is exhausted. It became a noisy place where every one is discussing. It became a war place where every one is out of their mind.

By the way, it's my classroom!

In the end of the day

It became a fish market where everyone is shouting on one another.

It became a dustbin where everyone left their things even their books.

It became a local market where everyone push each other to leave.

By the way, it's my classroom

9 798885 469692

Printed by Libri Plureos GmbH in Hamburg,
Germany